Hello, Boys! by Ella Wheeler Wilcox

Poetry is a fascinating use of language. With almost a million words at its command it is not surprising that these Isles have produced some of the most beautiful, moving and descriptive verse through the centuries. In this series we look at the world through the eyes and minds of our most gifted poets to bring you a unique poetic guide to their lives.

Born on November 5th 1850 in Johnstown, Wisconsin, Ella Wheeler was the youngest of four children. She began to write as a child and by the time she graduated was already well known as a poet throughout Wisconsin.

Regarded more as a popular poet than a literary poet her most famous work 'Solitude' reflects on a train journey she made where giving comfort to a distressed fellow traveller she wrote how the others grief imposed itself for a time on her 'Laugh and the world laughs with you, Weep and you weep alone'. It was published in 1883 and was immensely popular.

The following year, 1884, she married Robert Wilcox. They lived for a time in New York before moving to Connecticut. Their only child, a son, died shortly after birth. It was around this time they developed an interest in spiritualism which for Ella would develop further into an interest in the occult. In later years this and works on positive thinking would occupy much of her writing.

On Robert's death in 1916 she spent months waiting for word from him from 'the other side' which never came.

In 1918 she published her autobiography The Worlds And I.

Ella died of cancer on October 30th, 1919.

Index Of Poems
Forward
Thanksgiving
The Brave Highland Laddies
Men of the Sea
Ode to the British Fleet
The German Fleet
Deep Unto Deep Was Calling
The Song of the Allies
Ten Thousand Men a Day
"America Will Not Turn Back"
War
The Hour

The Message
"Flowers of France"
Our Atlas
Camp Followers
Come Back Clean
Camouflage
The Awakening
The Khaki Boys Who Were Not At the Front
Time's Hymn of Hate
Dear Motherland of France
The Spirit of Great Joan
Speak
The Girl of the U.S.A.
Passing the Buck
Song of the Aviator
The Stevedores
A Song of Home
The Swan of Dijon
Veils
In France I Saw a Hill
American Boys, Hello!
De Rochambeau
After
The Blasphemy of Guns
The Crimes of Peace
It May Be
Then and Now
Widows
Conversation
I, too
He That Hath Ears
Answers
How Is It?
'Let Us Give Thanks'
The Black Sheep
One By One
Prayer
Be Not Dismayed
Ascension
The Deadliest Sin
The Rainbow of Promise
They Shall Not Win
Ella Wheeler Wilcox – A Short Biography
Ella Wheeler Wilcox – A Concise Bibliography

FORWARD

The greater part of these verses dealing with the war were written in France during my recent seven months' sojourn there, and for the purpose of using in entertainments given in camps and hospitals to thousands of American soldiers.

They were the result of coming into close contact with the soldiers' mind and heart, and were intentionally expressed in the simplest manner, without any consideration of methods approved by modern critics. The fact that I have been asked to autograph scores of copies of many of these verses (and one of them to the extent of 350 copies) is more gratifying to me than would be the highest encomiums of the purely literary critic.

Ella Wheeler Wilcox
London, October 1918.

THANKSGIVING

Thanksgiving for the strong armed day,
That lifted war's red curse,
When Peace, that lordly little word,
Was uttered in a voice that stirred
Yea, shook the Universe.

Thanksgiving for the Mighty Hour
That brimmed the Victor's cup,
When England signalled to the foe,
'The German flag must be brought low
And not again hauled up!'

Thanksgiving for the sea and air
Free from the Devil's might!
Thanksgiving that the human race
Can lift once more a rev'rent face,
And say, 'God helps the Right.'

Thanksgiving for our men who came
In Heaven-protected ships,
The waning tide of hope to swell,
With 'Lusitania' and 'Cavell'
As watchwords on their lips.

Thanksgiving that our splendid dead,
All radiant with youth,
Dwell near to us, there is no death.
Thanksgiving for the broad new faith

That helps us know this truth.

THE BRAVE HIGHLAND LADDIES
I had seen our splendid soldiers in their khaki uniforms,
And their leaders with a Sam Brown belt;
I had seen the fighting Britons and Colonials in swarms,
I had seen the blue-clad Frenchmen, and I felt
That the mighty martial show
Had no new sight to bestow,
Till I walked on Piccadilly, and my word!
By the bonnie Highland laddies
In their kilts and their plaidies,
To a wholly new sensation I was stirred.

They were like some old-time picture, or a scene from out a play,
They were stalwart, they were young, and debonnair;
Their jaunty little caps they wore in such a fetching way,
And they showed their handsome legs, and didn't care
And they seemed to own the town
As they strode on up and down
Oh, they surely were a sight for tired eyes!
Those braw, bonnie laddies
In their kilts and their plaidies,
And I stared at them with pleasure and surprise.

I had read about the valour of old Scotland's warrior sons
How they fought to a finish, or else fell;
I had heard the name bestowed on them by agitated Huns,
Who called these skirted soldiers 'Dames of Hell';
And I gave them right of way
On their London holiday,
As I met them swinging down the street and Strand,
Those bonnie, bonnie laddies
In their kilts and their plaidies,
And I breathed a blessing on them and their land

Now the world is all rejoicing that the end of war has come
And no heart is any gladder than my own,
That the brutal, blatant voices of the guns at last are dumb,
And the Dove of Peace from out her cage has flown.
Yet, when men no more march by,
Making pictures for the eye,
There's a vital dash of colour earth will lack,
When the brave Highland laddies
Drop their kilts and their plaidies,
And return to common clothes of grey or black!

MEN OF THE SEA

Many the songs of the brave boys sent
Over The Top in the battle's thunder;
But mine is the song of the men who went
Over the top of the waves and under.

Men of the sea, Men of the sea,
I lift mine eyes to the Flags unfurled
The Flags of Victory blowing free
Over the new-born world.
And I cry 'Thank God! these things can be!
Thank God, and the Men of the Sea!'

Little it matters to what they belong,
Marine or Navy or Merchant Ship
To the Men of the Sea I sing my song;
A song that rises from heart to lip.

I sing of the valour that ploughed a path
Straight through the snares of a crafty foe,
Through billows raging with wintry wrath,
And over the dens of the devils below.

To the splendid heroes of Jutland Bank
And the Royal Navy I give their due;
And cheek by jowl with them all, I rank
The brave mine-sweepers and merchant crew.

Trawler, Drifter, or English Fleet
All are manned by the Men of the Sea,
And all together in my heart meet,
For a boat is a boat to the mind of me.

And who ever over the dread seas fared,
And however humble his work or place,
To the great Christ spirit must be compared
Since he offered his life for the good of the race.

And how many lie in the deep-sea bed,
No man can reckon, and no man number;
But not one Soul of them all is dead,
For death is only the body's slumber.

And the Men of the Mist, who from dark to dawn
On the deck or the bridge stand guard at night,

Oft feel the presence of comrades gone
Who keep watch with them, though veiled from sight.

Many the songs of the brave boys sent
Over The Top in the battle's thunder;
But mine is the song of the men who went
Over the top of the waves and under.

ODE TO THE BRITISH FLEET
'Invisible and silent' Mystery
Surrounded that great Guardian of the Sea.
That Father, Mother, of the mighty main.
While loud in valley and on field and hill
And over anguished plain
The battles thundered. God himself is still
And hidden from men's view; and it were meet
That this subliminal force
Should move in utter silence on its course
Invisible, Inaudible, till that hour
When Time, Fate's Minister, should speak and say
'Come forth! and show thy power!'
When Time commands, even the gods obey.

'Invisible and silent'; yet the foe
Was driven from the Sea. All impotent
The brazen braggart went.
While commerce sent her brave ships to and fro;
And from Columbia's shores there sailed away
Ten thousand men a day
Ten thousand men a day! who reached their goals
Bringing new courage to war-weary souls.

Oh, silent wonder of the noisy sea!
Though alien, with the blood of Bunker Hill
Down filtering through my veins, the heart of me
Seems with a mingled love and awe to fill
And overflow at thought of that sublime,
Unparalleled large hour of Time;
When bloodless Victory saw the foes' flag furled
That insolent menace to a righteous world.

Great Britain's Fleet unshaken in its might,
Proclaimed itself again in all men's sight
The Mistress of the Main. Fair Freedom's friend,
May peace and glory on thy path attend.

THE GERMAN FLEET

Lie down, and let the billows hide your shame,
Oh, shorn and naked outcast of the seas!
You who confided to each ocean breeze
Your coming conquests, and made loud acclaim
Of your own grandeur and exalted fame;
You who have catered to they world's disease;
You who have drunk hate's wine, and found the lees;
Lie down! and let all men forget your name!

You dreamed of world dominion! you! the spawn
Of hell and hatred, Foe to all things free
Sworn enemy to honour, truth and right;
Too poor a thing now for the Devil's pawn,
Let the large mercy of the outraged sea
Engulf and hide you evermore from sight.

DEEP UNTO DEEP WAS CALLING

They rode through the bannered city
The King and the Commoner,
And the hopes of the world were with them,
And the heart of the world was astir.
For the moss-grown walls seemed falling
That have shut away men from Kings;
And Deep unto Deep was calling
For the coming of greater things.

They rode to an age-old Palace
Where the feet of the Mighty go
(A Palace that stands unshaken
Despite the boast of the foe!)
And the King from Kings descending
And the Man of the People's choice
In a Super-Man seemed blending,
And they spoke as with one voice.

And one voice now and for ever
Will speak from sea to sea,
Wherever the British Banner
And the Starry Flag float free.
For our fettering chains are sundered
By the evil that turned to good,
And Deep unto Deep has thundered
Its message of Brotherhood.

It was not a pageant of Victors
Or a triumph hour of man,
That ride through the bannered City,
It was part of a Mighty Plan;
And the sound of old barriers falling
Rose there where those Rulers trod,
For Deep unto Deep was calling
In the resonant Voice of God.

THE SONG OF THE ALLIES
We are the Allies of God to-day,
And the width of the earth is our right of way.
Let no man question or ask us why,
As we speed to answer a wild world cry;
Let no man hinder or ask us where,
As out over water and land we fare;
For whether we hurry, or whether we wait,
We follow the finger of guiding fate.

We are the Allies. We differ in faith,
But are one in our courage at thought of death.
Many and varied the tongues we speak,
But one and the same is the goal we seek.
And the goal we seek is not power or place,
But the peace of the world, and the good of the race.
And little matters the colour of skin,
When each heart under it beats to win.

We are the Allies; we fight or fly,
We wallow in trenches like pigs in a sty,
We dive under water to foil a foe,
We wait in quarters, or rise and go.
And staying or going, or near or far,
One thought is ever our guiding star:
We are the Allies of God to-day,
We are the Allies, make way! make way!

TEN THOUSAND MEN A DAY
All the world was wearying,
All the world was sad;
Everything was shadow-filled;
Things were going bad.
Then a rumour stirred all hearts
As a wind stirs trees
Ten thousand men a day

Coming over seas!

Soon we saw them marching by
God! what a sight!
Shoulders back, and heads erect,
Faces full of light.
Smiling like a morn in May,
Moving like a breeze,
Ten thousand men a day
Coming over seas.

Weary soldiers worn with war
Lifted up their eyes,
Shadows seemed to fade a bit,
Dawn was in the skies.
Hope sprang to troubled hearts,
Strength to tired knees:
Ten thousand men a day
Were coming over seas.

France and England swarmed with them,
Khaki-clad and young,
Filled with all the joy of life
Into line they swung.
Waning valour rose anew
At the sight of these
Ten thousand men a day
Coming over seas.

Still they come and still they come
In their strength and pride.
Victory with radiant mien
Marches on beside.
Victory is here to stay,
Every heart agrees,
With ten thousand men a day
Coming over seas.

'AMERICA WILL NOT TURN BACK'
WOODROW WILSON

America will not turn back;
She did not idly start,
But weighed full carefully and well
Her grave, important part.
She chose the part of Freedom's friend,

And will pursue it, to the end.

Great Liberty, who guards her gates,
Will shine upon her course,
And light the long, adventurous path
With radiance from God's Source.
And though blood dye that ocean track,
America will not turn back.

She will not turn until that hour
When thunders through the world
The crash of tyrant monarchies
By Freedom's hand down-hurled.
While Labour's voice from sea to sea
Sings loud, 'My country, 'tis of thee.'

Then will our fair Columbia turn,
While all wars' clamours cease,
And with our banner lifted high
Proclaim, 'Let there be Peace.'
But till that glorious day shall dawn
She will march on, she will march on.

WAR

I
There is no picturesqueness and no glory,
No halo of romance, in war to-day.
It is a hideous thing; Time would turn grey
With horror, were he not already hoary
At sight of this vile monster, foul and gory.
Yet while sweet women perish as they pray,
And new-born babes are slaughtered, who dare say
'Halt!' till Right pens its 'Finis' to the story!
There is no pathway, but the path through blood,
Out of the horrors of this holocaust.
Hell has let loose its scalding crimson flood,
And he who stops to argue now is lost.
Not brooms of creeds, not Pacifistic words
Can stem the tide, but swords, uplifted swords!

II
Yet, after Peace has turned the clean white page
There shall be sorrow on the earth for years;
Abysmal grief, that has no eyes for tears,
And youth that hobbles through the earth like age.
But better to play this part upon life's stage

Than to aid structures that a tyrant rears,
To live a stalwart hireling torn with fears,
And shamed by feeding on a conqueror s wage.
Death, yea, a thousand deaths, were sweet in truth
Rather than such ignoble life. God gave
Being, and breath, and high resolve to youth
That it might be Wrong's master, not its slave.
Our road to Freedom is the road to guns!
Go, arm your sons! I say, Go, arm your sons!

III
Arm! arm! that mandate on each wind is whirled.
Let no man hesitate or look askance,
For from the devastated homes of France
And ruined Belgium the cry is hurled.
Why, Christ Himself would keep peace banners furled
Were He among us, till, with lifted lance,
He saw the hosts of Righteousness advance
To purify the Temples of the world.
There is no safety on the earth to-day
For any sacred thing, or clean, or fair;
Nor can there be, until men rise and slay
The hydra-headed monster in his lair.
War! horrid War! now Virtue's only friend;
Clasp hands with War, and battle to the end!

THE HOUR
This is the world's stupendous hour
The supreme moment for the race
To see the emptiness of power,
The worthlessness of wealth and place,
To see the purpose and the plan
Conceived by God for growing man.

And they who see and comprehend
That ultimate and lofty aim
Will wait in patience for the end,
Knowing injustice cannot claim
One lasting victory, or control
Laws that bar progress for the whole.

This is an epoch-making time;
God thunders through the universe
A message glorious and sublime,
At once a blessing and a curse.
Blessings for those who seek His light,

Curses for those whose law is might.

Ephemeral as the sunset glow
Is human grandeur. Mortal life
Was given that souls might seek and know
Immortal truths; and through the strife
That shakes the earth from land to land
The wise shall hear and understand.

Out of the awful holocaust,
Out of the whirlwind and the flood,
Out of old creeds to Bedlam tossed,
Shall rise a new earth washed in blood
A new race filled with spirit power,
This is the world's stupendous hour.

THE MESSAGE
I have not the gift of vision,
I have not the psychic ear,
And the realms that are called Elysian
I neither see nor hear;
Yet oft when the shadows darken
And the daylight hides its face,
The soul of me seems to hearken
For the truths that speak through space.

They speak to me not through reason,
They speak to me not by word;
Yet my soul would be guilty of treason
If it did not say it had heard.
For Space has a message compelling
To give to the ear of Earth;
And the things which the Silence is telling
In the bosom of God have birth.

Now this is the truth as I hear it
That ever through good or ill,
The will of the Ruling Spirit
Is moving and ruling still.
In the clutch of the blood-red terror
That holds the world in its might,
The Race is learning its error
And will find its way to the light.

And this is the Truth as I see it
Whoever cries out for peace,

Must think it, and live it, and BE IT,
And the wars of the world will cease.
Men fight that man may awaken,
And no longer want to kill;
Wars rage, and the heavens are shaken
That man may learn how to be still.

In the silence he finds his Saviour
The God Who is dwelling within;
And only by Christ-behaviour
Is the soul of him saved from sin.
There is only one Source, no other
One Light, and each soul is a ray;
And he who would slaughter his brother,
HIMSELF he is seeking to slay.

Now these are the Truths we are learning
Through evils and horrors untold;
For the thought of the race is turning
Away from its methods of old.
And the mind of the race is sated,
With the things that it prized of yore,
And the monster of war is hated,
As never on earth before.

Oh, slow are God's mills in the grinding,
But they grind exceedingly small;
And slow is man's soul in the finding,
That he is a part of the All.
Through aeons and aeons, his story
Is bloody and blackened with crime;
But he will come out into glory
And stand on the summits sublime.

He will stand on the summits of Knowledge,
In the splendour of Light from the Source;
And the methods of church and of college
Will all of them change by his force.
For the creeds that are blind and cruel,
And the teachings by rule and by rod,
Will all be turned into fuel
To light up the pathway to God.

This is the Truth as I hear it
The clouds are rolling away,
And Spirit will talk with Spirit
In the swift approaching day.

War from the world shall be driven,
From evil shall come forth good;
And men shall make ready for Heaven
Through living in Brotherhood.

'FLOWERS OF FRANCE'
DECORATION POEM FOR SOLDIERS' GRAVES, TOURS, FRANCE, MAY 30, 1918

Flowers of France in the Spring,
Your growth is a beautiful thing;
But give us your fragrance and bloom
Yea, give us your lives in truth,
Give us your sweetness and grace
To brighten the resting-place
Of the flower of manhood and youth,
Gone into the dust of the tomb.

This is the vast stupendous hour of Time,
When nothing counts but sacrifice and faith,
Service and self-forgetfulness. Sublime
And awful are these moments charged with death
And red with slaughter. Yet God's purpose thrives
In all this holocaust of human lives.

I say God's purpose thrives. Just in the measure
That men have flung away their lust for gain,
Stopped in their mad pursuit of worldly pleasure,
And boldly faced unprecedented pain
And dangers, without thinking of the cost,
So thrives God's purpose in the holocaust.

Death is a little thing: all men must die;
But when ideals die, God grieves in Heaven.
Therefore I think it was the reason why
This Armageddon to the world was given.
The Soul of man, forgetful of its birth,
Was losing sight of everything but earth.

Up from these many million graves shall spring,
A shining harvest for the coming race.
An Army of Invisibles shall bring
A glorified lost faith back to its place.
And men shall know there is a higher goal
Than earthly triumphs for the human soul.

They are not dead, they are not dead, I say,
These men whose mortal forms are in the sod.
A grand Advance-Guard marching on its way,
Their Souls move upwards to salute their God!
While to their comrades who are in the strife
They cry, 'Fight on! Death is the dawn of life.'

We had forgotten all the depth and beauty
And lofty purport of that old true word
Deplaced by pleasure, that old good word DUTY.
Now by its meaning is the whole world stirred.
These men died for it; for it, now, we give,
And sacrifice, and serve, and toil, and live.
From out our hearts had gone a high devotion
For anything. It took a mighty wrath
Against great evil to wake strong emotion,
And put us back upon the righteous path.
It took a mingled stream of tears and blood
To cut the channel through to Brotherhood.

That word meant nothing on our lips in peace:
We had despoiled it by our castes and classes.
But when this savage carnage finds surcease
A new ideal will unite the masses.
And there shall be True Brotherhood with men
The Christly Spirit stirring earth again.

For this our men have suffered, fought, and died.
And we who can but dimly see the end
Are guarded by their spirits glorified,
Who help us on our way, while they ascend.
They are not dead, they are not dead, I say,
These men whose graves we decorate to-day.

America and France walk hand in hand;
As one, their hearts beat through the coming years:
One is the aim and purpose of each land,
Baptized with holy water of their tears.
To-day they worship with one faith, and know
Grief's first Communion in God's House of Woe.

Great Liberty, the Goddess at our gates,
And great Jeanne d'Arc, are fused into one soul:
A host of Angels on that soul awaits
To lead it up to triumph at the goal.
Along the path of Victory they tread,
Moves the majestic cortege of our dead.

Flowers of France in the Spring,
Your growth is a beautiful thing;
But give us your fragrance and bloom
Yea, give us your lives in truth,
Give us your sweetness and grace
To brighten the resting-place
Of the flower of manhood and youth,
Gone into the dust of the tomb.

OUR ATLAS
Not Atlas, with his shoulders bent beneath the weighty world,
Bore such a burden as this man, on whom the Gods have hurled
The evils of old festering lands, yea, hurled them in their might
And left him standing all alone, to set the wrong things right.

It is the way the Fates have done since first Time's race began!
They open up Pandora's box before some chosen man;
And then, aloof, they wait and watch, to see if he will find
And wake the slumbering God that dwells in every mortal's mind.

Erect, our modern Atlas stands, with brave uplifted head,
And there is courage in his eyes, if in his heart be dread.
Not dread of foes, but dread of friends, who may not pull together,
To bring the lurching ship of State safe through the stormy weather.

Oh, never were there wilder waves or more stupendous seas,
Or rougher rocks or bleaker winds, or darker days than these.
Not Washington, not Lincoln knew so grave an hour of Time
As he who now stands face to face with War's world-shaking crime.

His brain is clear, his soul is brave, his heart is just and right,
He asks no honours of the earth, but favour in God's sight;
His aim is not to wear a crown or win imperial power,
But to use wisely for the race life's terrible great hour.

O Liberty, who lights the world with rays that come from God,
Shine on Columbia's troubled track, and make it bright and broad;
Shine on each heart, and give it strength to meet its pains and losses,
And give supernal strength to one who bears the whole world's crosses;
Take from his thought the fear of friends who may not pull together,
And bring the glorious ship of State safe through wild waves and weather.

CAMP FOLLOWERS
In the old wars of the world there were camp followers,
Women of ancient sins who gave themselves for hire,
Women of weak wills and strong desire.
And, like the poison ivy in the woods

That winds itself about tall virile trees
Until it smothers them, so these
Ruined the bodies and the souls of men.
More evil were they than Red War itself,
Or Pestilence, or Famine. Now in this war
This last most awful carnage of the world
All the old wickedness exists as then:

But as a foul stream from a festering fen
Is met and scattered by a mountain brook
Leaping along its beautiful, bright course,
So now the force
Of these new Followers of the camp has come
Straight from God's Source
To cleanse the world and cleanse the minds of men.
Good women, of great courage and large hearts,
Women whose slogan is self-sacrifice,
Willing to pay the price
God asks of pioneers, now play their parts
In this stupendous drama of the age
As Followers of the Camps.

They come in the name of God our Father,
They come in the name of Christ our Brother,
They come in the name of All Humanity,
To give their gold, their labour, and their love
To help the suffering souls in this war-riddled earth,
The New Women of the Race
The New Camp Followers
The Centuries shall do honour to their names.

COME BACK CLEAN
This is the song for a soldier
To sing as he rides from home
To the fields afar where the battles are
Or over the ocean's foam:
'Whatever the dangers waiting
In the lands I have not seen,
If I do not fall, if I come back at all,
Then I will come back clean.

'I may lie in the mud of the trenches,
I may reek with blood and mire,
But I will control, by the God in my soul,
The might of my man's desire.
I will fight my foe in the open,

But my sword shall be sharp and keen
For the foe within who would lure me to sin,
And I will come back clean.

'I may not leave for my children
Brave medals that I have worn,
But the blood in my veins shall leave no stains
On bride or on babes unborn;
And the scars that my body may carry
Shall not be from deeds obscene,
For my will shall say to the beast, OBEY!
And I will come back clean.

'Oh, not on the fields of slaughter
And not in the prison-cell,
Or in hunger and cold is the story told
By war, of its darkest hell.
But the old, old sin of the senses
Can tell what that word may mean
To the soldiers' wives and to innocent lives,
And I will come back clean.'

CAMOUFLAGE
Camouflage is all the rage.
Ladies in their fight with age
Soldiers in their fight with foes
Demagogues who mask and pose
In the guise of statesmen, girls
Black of eyes with golden curls
Politicians, votes in mind,
Smiling, affable and kind,
All use camouflage to-day.
As you go upon your way,
Walk with caution, move with care;
Camouflage is everywhere!

THE AWAKENING
I said, 'I will place my heart, my heart all broken,
Beside the world's torn heart, that it may know
The comradeship of sorrow that is not spoken,
But is carried on wings of all the winds that blow.
I will go homeless into homes of grieving,
And find my own grief easier to be borne.'
So over menacing seas I went, believing
Where all was mourning, I would cease to mourn.

And now I am here, close to the great world-sorrow,
Here where each heart some mighty grief has known;
But from each suffering soul I seem to borrow
A poignant pain that but augments my own.
The earth is like one vast tempestuous ocean,
Where struggling beings fight for light and breath:
I feel their anguish, feel each keen emotion -
Yet through it all, I KNOW THERE IS NO DEATH.

And as we toss on billows red with slaughter,
Unto each tortured, anguished soul I cry,
'There are green lands beyond this raging water,
We shall come into harbour by and by.
Our dead dwell near, life is a thing eternal:
And I have talked with One from that fair shore.
We are but passing through a dream infernal;
We shall awake, we shall be glad once more.'

THE KHAKI BOYS WHO WERE NOT AT THE FRONT

Oh! it is not just the men who face the guns,
Not the fighters at the Front alone, to-day
Who will bring the longed-for close to the bloody fray, for those
Could not carry on that fray without the ones
Who are working at war's problems far away.

You are ALL our splendid heroes in the strife,
And we class you with the warriors maimed and scarred,
Though you never have been near enough the battle din to hear,
While you laboured in the dull routine of life
In your khaki suits with sleeves that are not barred.

You have offered up yourselves to save the world;
You have felt the abnegation of the Christ:
And whatever work you do is a noble work and true;
Though it be not done with banners all unfurled,
You will find it has, in sight of God, sufficed.

While you carry back no medals when you go,
Not without you had the fighters borne war's brunt:
So just lift your heads uncowed, for your country will be proud
And its lasting love and honour will bestow
On the khaki boys who were not at the Front.

TIME'S HYMN OF HATE

Oh, boastful, wicked land, that once was beautiful and great,
How bitter and how black must be your self-invited fate,
While Time goes down the centuries and sings his hymn of hate!

Time's voice is just. His words ring true. For as the past recedes,
The clear-eyed Future slowly writes the story of its deeds;
And as Time toward the Infinite his ceaseless flight is winging
He shall go singing
The hymn of hate, of men and gods, for all your deeds of lust,
For all your acts of cruelty and hell-concocted schemes
(More hideous than the darkest plot of which a devil dreams)
Which sprang from your Medusa head before it touched the dust.

Beneath the strangling hand of Fate
That strident voice of yours
Shall hush to silence, soon or late
That Justice that endures
Will mobilise its mighty ranks and free the human race,
Then shall all Space,
Yea, all the chains of sphere on sphere,
With that loud hymn be ringing,
Which Time goes singing
His far flight winging
And all the cherubims of God that dwell in regions o'er us
Shall swell the chorus.

Oh, boastful, wicked land, that once was beautiful and great,
How desolate and dark must be your self-invited fate,
While Time goes down the centuries and sings his hymn of hate!

DEAR MOTHERLAND OF FRANCE
DEDICATED TO THE MEN AND WOMEN OF FRANCE

Our Motherland, dear Motherland,
The source of beauty and of Art,
Who but thy children understand
The love which permeates each heart!
We see, through rainbow-tints of tears,
Thy glory of a thousand years.
O country of the Great and Free,
We live for thee, we live for thee,
Dear Motherland of France.

O Motherland, both blithe and brave,
What magic lies in thy name, France!
Yet can thy radiant mien be grave,

And stern thy ever-smiling glance.
And when thy sons and daughters know
That enemies would lay thee low
And dim thy fame on land and sea,
We fight for thee, we fight for thee,
Dear Motherland of France.

Dear Motherland of joy and mirth,
Dear Motherland of faith divine,
A thousand years the wondering earth
Has seen thy star in splendour shine.
Still shall it see that star of France
Its splendour and its light enhance.
Dear Motherland, when it need be
We die for thee, we die for thee,
Dear Motherland of France.

THE SPIRIT OF GREAT JOAN
Back of each soldier who fights for France,
Ay, back of each woman and man
Who toils and prays through these long tense days,
Is the spirit of Great Joan.
For the love she gave, and the life she gave,
In the eyes of God sufficed
To crown her with light, and power, and might,
That made her second to Christ.

And so in that hour at the Marne she came,
To the seeing eyes of men;
And the blind of view still felt and knew
That her spirit had come again.
And she will come in each crucial hour
And joy shall follow despair,
For Joan sees her France on its knees
And she hears the voice of its prayer.

There is no hate in the heart of France,
But a mighty moral force
That takes its stand for her worshipped land,
And cannot be swerved from its course.
For this is the way with France to-day,
Her courage comes from faith,
And she bends her knee ere she straightens her arm;
In her forward rush toward death.

A jungle of beasts in the heart of the Hun

War to the world laid bare.
And war has revealed, that France concealed,
Only the lion's lair.
A lioness fighting to save her own,
She fights as a lioness can,
And strength to the end shall the Unseen send,
In the spirit of Great Joan.

SPEAK
Obscured the sun, the world is dark;
Maid of Orleans, Joan of Arc,
Send down thy spark.

Let every heart in France be stirred,
By such an all-compelling word
As thou once heard.

Say to each soul, 'Lo! I am near;
My voice still speaks in accents clear.
Be still and hear.

'The France I saved cannot be lost;
Though tempest-torn and terror-tossed,
Count not the cost.

'Give as the maid of Domremy
Gave all, gave life itself to see
Her country free.

'Back of great France my spirit towers
To aid her through the darkest hours
With God's own powers!'

Maid of Orleans, Joan of Arc,
Shine through the night, speak through the dark
The while we hark.

THE GIRL OF THE U.S.A.
Oh! the maidens of France are certainly fine,
And I think every fellow will state
That the 'what-you-may-call-it' coiffured way
They put up their hair is great!
And they know how to dress, and they wear their clothes
In a fetching, Frenchy way;
And yet to me, there is just one girl

The girl of the U.S.A.

I like to listen when French girls talk,
Though I'm weak in the 'parlez-vous' game;
But the language of youth in every land
Is somehow about the same,
And I've learned a regular code of shrugs,
And they seem to know what I say!
But the girl whose voice goes straight to my heart
Is the girl of the U.S.A.

I haven't a word but words of praise
For these dear little girls of France;
And I will confess that I've felt a thrill
As I faced their line of advance!
But I haven't been taken a prisoner yet,
And I won't be, until the day
When I carry my colours to lay at the feet
Of a girl of the U.S.A.

PASSING THE BUCK
Whatever the task that comes your way,
Just take it as part of your luck.
Look it right square in the eyes, and say,
'This is MY task, I'll do it to-day':
Don't pass the buck.

Oh! whether you cook, or whether you fight,
Or whether you trundle a truck,
Just tackle your job and do it right:
Don't pass the buck.

The wheels of the earth have gone, alack!
Deep into war's mire and muck.
If you want to put it again on its track,
Don't shift your load on another man's back:
Don't pass the buck.

SONG OF THE AVIATOR
You may thrill with the speed of your thoroughbred steed,
You may laugh with delight as you ride the ocean,
You may rush afar in your touring car,
Leaping, sweeping, by things that are creeping
But you never will know the joy of motion
Till you rise up over the earth some day,

And soar like an eagle, away, away.

High and higher above each spire,
Till lost to sight is the tallest steeple,
With the winds you chase in a valiant race,
Looping, swooping, where mountains are grouping,
Hailing them comrades, in place of people.
Oh! vast is the rapture the birdman knows,
As into the ether he mounts and goes.
He is over the sphere of human fear;
He has come into touch with things supernal.
At each man's gate death stands await;
And dying, flying, were better than lying
In sick-beds, crying for life eternal.
Better to fly half-way to God
Than to burrow too long like a worm in the sod.

THE STEVEDORES

We are the army stevedores, lusty and virile and strong,
We are given the hardest work of the war, and the hours are long.
We handle the heavy boxes, and shovel the dirty coal;
While soldiers and sailors work in the light, we burrow below like a mole.
But somebody has to do this work, or the soldiers could not fight!
And whatever work is given a man, is good if he does it right.

We are the army stevedores, and we are volunteers.
We did not wait for the draft to come, to put aside our fears;
We flung them away on the winds of fate, at the very first call of our land,
And each of us offered a willing heart and the strength of a brawny hand.
We are the army stevedores, and work as we must and may,
The cross of honour will never be ours to proudly wear away.

But the men at the Front could never be there,
And the battles could not be won,
If the stevedores stopped in their dull routine
And left their work undone.
Somebody has to do this work; be glad that it isn't you!
We are the army stevedores, give us our due!

A SONG OF HOME

I am singing a song to the boys to-day,
A song of the home that is far away.

And I know that an echo the word is waking
In many a heart that is secretly aching,
Yes, almost breaking, thinking of Home, dear Home.
But thought, dear boys, is a carrier dove,
And it flies straight into the hearts you love.

You picture the days of your youthful joys,
The old home circle, the girls and boys
You knew in that wonderful world of pleasure,
When life danced on to a lilting measure;
Each scene you treasure, thinking of Home, dear Home.
And here is a thought that is sweet and true
The ones you long for are longing for you.
You picture the day when the war is done,
The duty accomplished, the victory won,
And over the billows our ships go leaping,
Into our beautiful harbour sweeping,
And with laughter and weeping, you go back Home, Home, Home.
On the walls of your heart you must hang with care
This beautiful picture, framed in prayer.

Thinking of Home, you are blazing a trail
For that glorious day when our ships shall sail;
Where the Goddess of Liberty lights the water
To guide you back from the fields of slaughter,
Fair Freedom's daughter, who welcomes us Home, Home, Home.
So hold your vision, and work and pray,
As you dream of the Home that is far away.

THE SWAN OF DIJON
I was in Dijon when the war's wild blast
Was at its loudest; when there was no sound
From dawn to dawn, save soldiers marching past,
Or rattle of their wagons in the street.
When every engine whistle would repeat
Persistently, with meaning tense, profound,
'We carry men to slaughter' or 'we bring
Remnants of men back as war's offering.'

And there in Dijon, the out-gazing eye
Grew weary of the strife-suggesting scene;
But, searching, found one quiet spot hard by
Where war was not; a little lake whereon
Moved leisurely a stately, tranquil swan,
Majestic and imposing, yet serene.

I was in Dijon, when no sound or sight
Woke thoughts of peace, save this one speck of white,
Sailing 'neath skies of menace, unafraid
While silver fountains for his pleasure played.
Dear Swan of Dijon, it was your good part
To rest a tired heart.

VEILS

Veils, everywhere float veils; veils long and black,
Framing white faces, oft-times young and fair,
But, like a rose touched by untimely frost,
Showing the blighting marks of sorrow's track.

Veils, veils, veils everywhere. They tell the cost
Of man-made war. They show the awful toll
Paid by the hearts of women for the crimes,
The age-old crimes by selfishness ill-named
'Justice' and 'Honour' and 'The call of Fate'
High words men use to hide their low estate.
About the joy and beauty of this world
A long black veil is furled.
Even the face of Heaven itself seems lost
Behind a veil. It takes a fervent soul
In these tense times
To visualise a God so long defamed
By insolent lips, that send out prayers, and prate
Of God's collaboration in dark deeds,
So foul they put to shame the fiends of hell.

Yet One DOES dwell
In Secret Centres of the Universe
The Mighty Maker; and He hears and heeds
The still small voice of soulful, selfless faith;
And He is lifting now the veil of death,
So long down-dropped between those worlds and earth.
Yea! He is giving faith a great new birth
By letting echoes from the hidden places
Where dwell our dead, fall on love's listening ear.
Hearken, and you shall hear
The messages which come from those star-spaces!
That is the reason why
God let so many die;
That the vast hordes of suffering hearts might wake
Mighty vibrations, and the silence break
Between the neighbouring worlds, and lift the veil
'Twixt life on earth, and life Beyond. All hail

To great Jehovah, Who has given life
Eternal, everlasting, after strife!

Veils, long black veils, you shall be bridal white.
Eyes, blind with tears, you shall receive your sight,
And see your dead alive in Worlds of Light.

IN FRANCE I SAW A HILL

In France I saw a hill, a gentle slope
Rising above old tombs to greet the gleam
From soft spring skies. Beyond these skies dwells hope,
But those green graves bespeak a broken dream.

There was a row of narrow beds, new-made;
Each bore a starry banner and a cross.
And each the name of one who, ere he played
His role of warrior, met earth's final loss.

They were so young, so eager for the fray!
And thoughts of glory filled each boyish heart,
When over dangerous seas they sailed away
To face the foe and play some splendid part.

But in the tedious toil, the dull routine
Which must precede achievement on the field,
Disease, that secret enemy with mean
Sly tactics, forced them to disarm and yield.

So they were buried on that hill in France,
Before their ears had heard the battle din;
Before life gave them its dramatic chance
A lasting fame, or glorious death to win.

Yet, looking up beyond their graves of green,
I seem to see them wearing band and star;
Men are rewarded in the Worlds Unseen
Not for the way they die, but what they are.

AMERICAN BOYS, HELLO!

Oh! we love all the French, and we speak in French
As along through France we go.
But the moments to us that are keen and sweet
Are the ones when our khaki boys we meet,
Stalwart and handsome and trim and neat;
And we call to them, 'Boys, hello!'

'Hello, American boys,
Luck to you, and life's best joys!
American boys, hello!'

We couldn't do that if we were at home
It never would do, you know!
For there you must wait till you're told who's who,
And to meet in the way that nice folks do.
Though you knew his name, and your name he knew
You never would say 'Hello, hello, American boy!'
But here it's just a joy,
As we pass along in the stranger throng,
To call out, 'Boys, hello!'

For each is a brother away from home;
And this we are sure is so,
There's a lonesome spot in his heart somewhere,
And we want him to feel there are friends RIGHT THERE
In this foreign land, and so we dare
To call out 'Boys, hello!'
'Hello, American boys,
Luck to you, and life's best joys!
American boys, hello!'

DE ROCHAMBEAU
ON THE PRESENTATION OF AN AMERICAN BANNER TO CAMP ROCHAMBEAU BY THE MARQUISE DE ROCHAMBEAU AT TOURS, FRANCE, JUNE 1, 1918

Here is a picture I carry away
On memory's wall. A green June day,
A golden sun in an amethyst sky,
And a beautiful banner floating as high
As the lofty spires of the city of Tours,
And a slender Marquise, with a face as pure
As a sculptured saint: while staunch and true
In new-world khaki and old-world blue,
Wearing their medals with modest pride,
Her stalwart bodyguard stand at her side.

Simple the picture; but much it may mean
To one who reads into and under the scene,
For there, in that opulent hour and weather,
Two great Republics came closer together;
A little nearer came land to land
Through the magical touch of a woman's hand.
And once again as in long ago
The grand old name of de Rochambeau

Shines forth like a star, for our world to see -
Our Land of the Brave, and our Home of the Free.

AFTER
Over the din of battle,
Over the cannons' rattle,
Over the strident voices of men and their dying groans,
I hear the falling of thrones.

Out of the wild disorder
That spreads from border to border,
I see a new world rising from ashes of ancient towns;
And the rulers wear no crowns.

Over the blood-charged water,
Over the fields of slaughter,
Down to the hidden vaults of Time, where lie the worn-out things,
I see the passing of kings.

THE BLASPHEMY OF GUNS
There must be lonely moments when God feels
The need of prayer
Such lonely moments, knowing not anywhere,
In any spot or place,
In all the far recesses of vast space,
Dwells any one to whom His prayers may rise,
And then, methinks, so urgent is His need
God bids His prayers descend.
He that has ears to hear, let him take heed,
For much God's prayers portend.

God flings His solar system forth to be
Finished by beings who befit each sphere.
Not ours to pry the secrets out of Mars;
Our work lies here.
To star-folk leave the stars.
There must be many worlds that give God care:
Young worlds that glow and burn,
Old worlds that freeze and fade.
This world is man's concern.
Methinks God must be very much dismayed,
Seeing the use we make of earth to-day,
While loud we pray.

Last night, in sleep, beyond the earth's small zone,

Adventurously my spirit went alone,
Past lesser hells and heavens, where souls may pause
To learn the meaning of death's larger laws,
Past astral shapes and bodies of desire,
Past angels and archangels, high and higher,
Until the pinnacles of space it trod,
Then, awestruck, paused, hearing the voice of God.

'Mortals of earth, for whom I shaped a sphere
(So spake the Voice), 'there rises to Mine ear
Eternal praises and eternal pleas.
Now, after centuries, I tire of these.
Have ye no knowledge of the Maker's needs,
Ye who ask favours and who praise by creeds?

Why has it not sufficed
That unto this small earth I sent great Christ,
Divine expression of the mortal man,
To aid my plan?

'Why ask for more when all has been refused?
Why praise My name Who hourly am abused?
Why seek for Me or heaven, when in you dwells
Hate's lurid hells?

'Persistent praises and persuasive pleas
I tire, I tire of these;
But I, the Maker of a billion suns,
Ask men to stop the blasphemy of guns.'
This is God's prayer.

(There must be many worlds that give God care.)

THE CRIMES OF PEACE
Musing upon the tragedies of earth,
Of each new horror which each hour gives birth,
Of sins that scar and cruelties that blight
Life's little season, meant for man's delight,
Methought those monstrous and repellent crimes
Which hate engenders in war-heated times,
To God's great heart bring not so much despair
As other sins which flourish everywhere
And in all times, bold sins, bare-faced and proud,
Unchecked by college, and by Church allowed,
Lifting their lusty heads like ugly weeds
Above wise precepts and religious creeds,

And growing rank in prosperous days of peace.
Think you the evils of this world would cease
With war's cessation?
If God's eyes know tears,
Methinks He weeps more for the wasted years
And the lost meaning of this earthly life
This big, brief life, than over bloody strife.
Yea; there are mean, lean sins God must abhor
More than the fatted, blood-drunk monster, War.
Looking from His place, looking from His high place among the stars,
God saw a peaceful land
A land of fertile fields and golden harvests and great cities whose innumerable spires pierced the vault of heaven, like bayonets of an invading army.
And God said, speaking unto Himself aloud, God said:
'Peace and power and plenty have I given unto this land; and those tall steeples are monuments to Me.
Now let My people reveal themselves, that I may see their works, done in My name in a fertile land of peace.
I will withdraw Mine eyes from other worlds that I may behold them, that I may behold these people to whom I sent Christ, they whose innumerable spires pierce My blue vault like bayonets.'
God saw the restless, idle rich in club and cabaret,
Meat-gorged, wine-filled, they played and preened and danced till dawn o' day;
They played at sports; they played at love; they played at being gay.
They were but empty, silk-clad shells; their souls had leaked away.
He saw the sweat-shop and the mill where little children toiled,
The sunless rooms where mothers slaved and unborn souls were spoiled;
While those whose greedy, selfish lives had thrust the toilers there,
He saw whirled down broad avenues, clothed all with raiment fair.

He saw in homes made beautiful with all that gold can give
Unhappy souls at odds with life, not knowing how to live.
He saw fair, pampered women turn from motherhood's sweet joy,
Obsessed with methods to prevent or mania to destroy.
He saw men sell their souls to vice and avarice and greed;
He heard race quarrelling with race and creed decrying creed;
And shameful wealth and waste He saw, and shameful want and need.

He saw bold little children come from church and schoolroom, blind
To suffering of lesser things, unfeeling and unkind;
He heard them taunt the poor, and tease their furred and feathered kin;

And no voice spake from home or church to tell them this was sin.
He heard the cry of wounded things, the wasteful gun's report;
He saw the morbid craze to kill, which Christian men called sport.

And then God hid His grieving face behind a wall of cloud,
On earth they said, 'A thunder-storm', but God had wept aloud.

IT MAY BE
Let us be silent for a little while;
Let us be still and listen. We may hear
Echoes from other worlds not far a way.

City on city rising, steeple out-topping steeple,
Gaining and hoarding and spending, and armies on battle bent,
People and people and people, and ever more human people
This is not all of creation, this is not all that was meant!
Earth on its orbit spinning,
This is not end or beginning;
That is but one of a trillion spheres out into the ether hurled:
We move in a zone of wonder,
And over our planet and under
Are infinite orders of beings and marvels of world on world.

There may be moving among us curious people and races,
Folk of the fourth dimension, folk of the vast star spaces.
They may be trying to reach us,
They may be longing to teach us
Things we are longing to know.
If it is so,
Voices like these are not heard in earth's riot,
Let us be quiet.

Classes with classes disputing, nation warring with nation,
Building and owning and seeking to lead, this is not all!
Endless the works of creation,
There may be waiting our call
Beings in numberless legions,
Dwellers in rarefied regions,
Journeying Godward like us,
Alist for a word to be spoken,
Awatch for a sign or a token.
If it be thus,
How they must grieve at our riotous noise
And the things we call duties and joys!

Let us be silent for a little while;

Let us be still and listen. We may hear
Echoes from other worlds not far away.

THEN AND NOW

A little time agone, a few brief years,
And there was peace within our beauteous borders;
Peace, and a prosperous people, and no fears
Of war and its disorders.
Pleasure was ruling goddess of our land; with her attendant Mirth
She led a jubilant, joy-seeking band about the riant earth.

Do you recall those laughing days, my Brothers,
And those long nights that trespassed on the dawn?
Those throngs of idle dancing maids and mothers
Who lilted on and on
Card mad, wine flushed, bejewelled and half stripped,
Yet women whose sweet mouth had never sipped
From sin's black chalice, women good at heart
Who, in the winding maze of pleasure's mart,
Had lost the sun-kissed way to wholesome pleasures of an earlier day.

Oh! You remember them! You filled their glasses;
You 'cut in' at their games of bridge; you left
Your work to drop in on their dancing classes
Before the day was cleft
In twain by noontide. When the night waxed late
You led your partner forth to demonstrate
The newest steps before a cheering throng,
And Time and Peace danced by your side along.

Peace is a lovely word, and we abhor that red word 'War';
But look ye, Brothers, what this war has done for daughters and for son,
For manhood and for womanhood, whose trend
Seemed year on year toward weakness to descend.
Upon this woof of darkness and of terror, woven by human error,
Behold the pattern of a new race-soul,
And it shall last while countless ages roll.

At the loud call of drums, out of the idler and the weakling comes
The hero valiant with self-sacrifice, ready to pay the price
War asks of men, to help a suffering world.
And out of the arms of pleasure, where they whirled
In wild unreasoning mirth, behold the splendid women of the earth
Living new selfless lives, the toiling mothers, sister, daughters,

wives
Of men gone forth as target for the foe.

Ah, now we know
Man is divine; we see the heavenly spark
Shining above the smoke and gloom and dark
Which was not visible in peaceful days.
God! wondrous are Thy ways,
For out of chaos comes construction; out of darkness and of doubt
And the black pit of death comes glorious faith;
From want and waste comes thrift, from weakness strength and power
And to the summits men and women lift
Their souls from self-indulgence in this hour,
This crucial hour of life:
So shines the golden side of this black shield of strife.

WIDOWS
The world was widowed by the death of Christ:
Vainly its suffering soul for peace has sought
And found it not.
For nothing, nothing, nothing has sufficed
To bring back comfort to the stricken house
From whence has gone the Master and the Spouse.

In its long widowhood the world has striven
To find diversion. It has turned away
From the vast aweful silences of Heaven
(Which answer but with silence when we pray)
And sought for something to assuage its grief.
Some surcease and relief
From sorrow, in pursuit of mortal joys.
It drowned God's stillness in a sea of noise;
It lost God's presence in a blur of forms;
Till, bruised and bleeding with life's brutal storms,
Unto immutable and speechless space
The World lifts up its face,
Its haggard, tear-drenched face,
And cries aloud for faith's supreme reward,
The promised Second Coming of its Lord.

So many widows, widows everywhere,
The whole earth teems with widows. Guns that blare -
Winged monsters of the air -
And deep-sea monsters leaping through the water,
Hell bent on slaughter,
All these plough paths for widows. Maids at dawn,

And brides at noon, ere eventide pass on
Into the ranks of widows: but to weep
Just for a little space; then will grief sleep
In their young bosoms, where sweet hope belongs,
New love will sing once more its age-old songs,
And life bloom as a rose-tree blooms again
After a night of rain.
There are complacent widows clothed in crepe
Who simulate a grief that is not real.
Through paths of seeming sorrow they escape
From disappointed hopes to some ideal,
Or, from the penury of unloved wives
Walk forth to opulent lives.
And there are widows who shed all their tears
Just at the first
In one wild burst,
And then go lilting lightly down the years:
Black butterflies, they flit from flower to flower
And live in the thin pleasures of the hour;
Merging their tender memories of the dead
In tenderer dreams of being once more wed.

But there are others: women who have proved
That loving greatly means so being loved.
Women who through full beauteous years have grown
Into the very body, souls, and heart
Of their dear comrades. When death tears apart
Such close-knit bonds as these, and one alone
Out to the larger freer life is called,
And one is left -
Then God in heaven must sometimes be appalled
At the wild anguish of the soul bereft,
And unto His Son must say, 'I did not know
Mortals could suffer so.'

But Christ, remembering Gethsemane,
Will answer softly, 'It was known to Me.'
God's alchemist, old Time, will merge to calm
That bitter anguish; but there is no balm
Save the sweet certitude that each long day
Is one step in a stair
That circles up to where freed spirits stay.

Widows, so many widows everywhere.

The world was widowed by the death of Christ,
And nothing, nothing, nothing has sufficed

To bring back comfort to the stricken house
From whence has gone the Master and the Spouse.
Hasten, dear Lord, with Thy Millennium, Hasten and come.

CONVERSATION
We were a baker's dozen in the house, six women and six men
Besides myself; and all of us had known
Those benefits supposed to come from school and church and brush and pen,
And opportunities of being thrown
In contact with the cultured and the gifted people of the day.
Being the thirteenth one among six pairs
I deemed it wise to keep apart and let the others have their say:
And from my vantage-place upon the stairs,
Or in a corner, where I seemed to read, I listened for some word
That would make life seem sweeter, or cast light
Upon the goal toward which all footsteps wend: and this was what I heard
Throughout each day and half of every night.
The men talked business, politics, and trade;
They told of safe investments, and great chances
For speculation. (One man who had made
Pleasure his art, described the newest dances
And dwelt upon each chasse, glide, and whirl
As lovers dwell upon the charms of some fair girl.)

They talked of war, and tried to find its cause,
And quite deplored the fact that wars must come.
But since this desperate condition was,
They carefully computed what the sum
Of profit might be to a land of peace,
And wondered if times would be harder should war cease.

They spoke of games and sports; told many a story
That made the listeners laugh; then back from these
Always they harked to money, or the gory
And savage drama playing overseas.
Then there were tales from club and smoking-room -
The submarines of gossip, bringing some name doom.

The women talked of fashions and of plays,
But more of players and their private lives;
Related tittle-tattle of their words and ways,
Their lightning change of husbands and of wives.
And there was chat of garments and their price,
Of operas and balls and all that gives life spice.

Some talk there was of music, pictures, books,
But of musicians, painters, authors, more.
The way they lived, their methods and their looks
The colour of their eyes, the clothes they wore;
And whether it was true, as had been stated,
That gifted people were quite sure to be mis-mated.

They talked of servants, menus, and disease,
And operations. Each one came in line
With some astounding tale to tell of these,
And of her surgeon's skill, which seemed divine.
But of that vast Domain where live our dead
And where we all are hurrying, no word was said.

When we know that goal awaits each one of us a little farther on,
When we know how an ever-increasing company of friends is gathered there,
Why do we not speak of it in our daily conversation?
Why do we not familiarise our minds with thoughts of worlds unseen?
There are many beautiful things to be learned of that country.
There are sacred books of great travellers, whose souls have cried,
'Hail across the border';

There are truths which have been learned in visions and by revelations:
All the revelations were not given to St. John alone,
All the wise men of the world did not die two thousand years ago!
Why do we not talk of these eternal truths,
Instead of wasting all our words on the evanesent, the ever-changing, the trivial, and the unimportant?
There is but one important theme, and that is Life Immortal.

I, TOO
I saw fond lovers in that glow
That oft-times fades away too soon:
I saw and said, 'Their joy I know -
I, too, have had my honeymoon.'

A young expectant mother's gaze
Held earth and heaven within its scope:
My thoughts went back to holy days -
I said, 'I, too, have known that hope.'

I saw a stricken mother swayed
By sorrow's storm, like wind-blown grass:

I said, 'I, too, dismayed
Have seen the little white hearse pass.'

I saw a matron rich with years
Walk radiantly beside her mate:
I blessed them, and said through my tears,
'I, too, have known that high estate.'

I saw a woman swathed in black
So blind with grief she could not see:
I said, 'Not far need I look back -
I, too, have known Gethsemane.'

I saw a face so full of light,
It seemed with all God's truths to shine:
I said, 'I, too, have found my sight,
I, too, have touched the Fact Divine.'

HE THAT HATH EARS

'He that hath an ear, let him hear what the Spirit saith unto the churches.' St. John the Divine.

The Spirit says unto the churches,
'Ere ever the churches began
I lived in the centre of Being
The life of the Purpose and Plan;
I flowed from the mind of the Maker
Through nature to man.

'I sleep in the glow of the jewel,
I wake in the sap of the tree,
I stir in the beast of the forest,
I reason in man, and am free
To turn on the path of Ascension
To the god yet to be.

'I was, and I am, and I will be;
I live in each church and each faith
But yield to no bond and no fetter,
I animate all with my breath;
I speak through the voice of the living
And I speak after death.'

The Spirit says unto the churches,
'The dead are not gone, they are near
And my voice, when I will it, speaks through them,

Speaks through them in messages clear.
And he that hath ears, in the silence
May listen and hear.'

The Spirit says unto the churches,
'So many the feet that have trod
The road leading up into knowledge,
The steep narrow path has grown broad;
And the curtain held down by old dogmas
Is lifted by God.'

ANSWERS

What is the end of each man's toil,
Brother, O Brother?
A handful of dust in a bit of soil
His name forgotten as centuries roll,
Though blazoned to-day on Glory's scroll;
For the lordliest work of brain or hand
Is only an imprint made on sand;
When the tidal wave sweeps over the shore
It is there no more,
Brother, my Brother.

Then what is the use of striving at all,
Brother, O Brother?
Because each effort or great or small
Is a step on the long, long road that leads
To the Kingdom of Growth on the River of Deeds:
And that is the kingdom no man can gain
Till he uses his hand and his mind and brain,
And when he has used them and learned control
He finds his soul,
Brother, my Brother.

And after he finds it, what is the end,
Brother, O Brother?
Upward ever its course and trend;
For this is the purpose and aim and plan
To seek in the soul for the Super-man
The man who is conscious that Heaven is near
A bulletin bearer from There to Here,
Finding God dwells in the spirit within
Where He ever has been,
Brother, my Brother.

And what will the God-man do when He comes,

Brother, O Brother?
He will better the world or in courts or slums,
He will do in gladness his nearest duty:
He will teach the religion of love and beauty
In field or factory, mine or mart,
While He tells the world of the larger part
And the wider life that is yet to be
When spirit is free,
Brother, my Brother.

When spirit is free, then where will it go,
Brother, O Brother?
Its uttermost summit no man may know,
For it goes up to God in His holy Tower
To gather more knowledge and force and power;
Like a ray of the sun it shall shine again
To brighten new planets and races of men.
Life had no beginning, life has no end,
Brother and friend -
Brother, my Brother.

HOW IS IT?

You who are loudly crying out for peace,
You who are wanting love to vanquish hate,
How is it in the four walls of your home
The while you wait?

Do those who form your household welcome your approach in the morning
As the earth welcomes the presence of dawn,
Or do they dread your coming lest you censure and complain?
Do you begin the day with praise to God for each blessing you possess, and do you speak frequent words of commendation to those about you?
Do those you claim to love often hear you talking in love's language,
Or is your softest tone and your sweetest speech saved for the sometime guest,
While the harsh voice and the sharp retort are used with those you love the best?

You who are praying for the Christ's return
And for the coming of the Promised Day,
How is it in the four walls of your home
The while you pray?

Are you trying to make your home a reflection of what you believe heaven will be?
Unless you are you will never find heaven anywhere;
The foundations of our heavenly mansions must first be built on earth.
Unless you are striving to put in use some of the angelic virtues here and now,
No angelhood will be accorded you hereafter.

Unless you are illustrating your desire for peace by a peaceful, love-ruled home,
You have no right to clamour for a cessation of hostilities among nations;
Nations are only chains of individuals.
When each individual expresses nothing but love and peace in his daily life, there will be no more war.

You who are loudly crying out for peace,
You who are wanting love to vanquish hate,
How is it in the four walls of your home
The while you wait?

'LET US GIVE THANKS'

For the courage which comes when we call,
While troubles like hailstones fall;
For the help that is somehow nigh,
In the deepest night when we cry;
For the path that is certainly shown
When we pray in the dark alone,
Let us give thanks.

For the knowledge we gain if we wait
And bear all the buffets of fate;
For the vision that beautifies sight
If we look under wrong for the right;
For the gleam of the ultimate goal
That shines on each reverent soul:
Let us give thanks.

For the consciousness stirring in creeds
That love is the thing the world needs;
For the cry of the travailing earth
That is giving a new faith birth;
For the God we are learning to find
In the heart and the soul and the mind:
Let us give thanks.

For the growth of the spirit through pain,
Like a plant in the soil and the rain;
For the dropping of needless things
Which the sword of a sorrow brings;
For the meaning and purpose of life
Which dawns on us out of the strife:
Let us give thanks.

For the solace that comes to our grief
In knowing earth's season is brief;
For the certitude given by faith
Of the continents out beyond death;
For the glorious thought that each day
Is speeding us the reward away:
Let us give thanks.

THE BLACK SHEEP
'Black sheep, black sheep, have you any wool?'
Yes, sir, yes, sir: three bags full.'

'I don't want any New Thought,' said he,
'Or any Theosophy, for, you see,
The faith I learned at my mother's knee
Is good enough for me.
Of course, I'm a wee bit broader than she,
Hearing one sermon where she heard three,
And I read my paper on Sunday, instead
Of the Bible only. My mother said
I was a black sheep, when she saw
I strayed a trifle away from the law,
And didn't think every one left in the lurch
Who happened to go to a different church;
But, still, in the main, her creed is mine,
And I don't want anything more divine.'
Yet his mother's mother was more austere;
She taught her children a creed of fear,
And she called them 'black sheep' when, with a shock,
She saw them straying away from the flock,
Just far enough
To get around places they thought too rough,
Like infant damnation and endless hell.

But his mother's mother's mother would tell
How her mother thought it was God's sweet will
To punish and torture a heretic till

They drove out the devil that made him dare
Think for himself in the matter of prayer
And faith and salvation. So we see how it is
If we look back over the centuries -
The creeds men learned at their mother's knee
When Salem witches were hanged to a tree,
And the pious dames flocked thither to see,
Are not deemed Christian or holy to-day;
And the bold black sheep who went straying away
From rut-worn paths in their search for God,
And leaped over the fence into pastures broad,
Are the great trail-makers for mortal souls,
Leading the race up to higher goals
And a larger religion; where man must find
God dwelling ever within his mind,
Christ in his conduct, and heaven in his thought,
And hell but the places where love is not.
A mighty religion that makes this earth
But the cradle that fits us for death's new birth
And the life beyond it, that is so near
Its echoes may reach to the listening ear.

'Black sheep, black sheep, have you any wool?'
'Yes, sir, yes, sir: a whole world full.'

ONE BY ONE
Little by little and one by one,
Out of the ether, were worlds created;
Star and planet and sea and sun,
All in the nebulous Nothing waited
Till the Nameless One Who has many a name
Called them to being and forth they came.

All things mighty and all things small,
Stone and flower and sentient being,
Each is an answer to that one call,
A part of Himself that His will is freeing
Freeing to go on the long, long way
That winds back home at the end of the day.

Little by little does mortal man
Build his castles for joy and glory,
And one by one time shatters each plan
And lowers his palaces, story by story
Story by story, till earth is just
A row of graves in the lowly dust.

One by one, whatever was called,
Must be called back to the primal Centre.
Let no soul tremble or be appalled,
For the heart of the Maker is where we enter
Is where we enter to gain new force
Before we are sent on another course.

And one by one, as He calls us back,
We shall find the souls that we loved with passion,
In the great way-stations along the track,
And clasp them again in the old, sweet fashion
In the old, sweet fashion when earth we trod
And journey along with them up to God.

PRAYER
Lord, let us pray.

Give us the open mind, O God,
The mind that dares believe
In paths of thought as yet untrod;
The mind that can conceive
Large visions of a wider way
Than circumscribes our world to-day.

May tolerance temper our own faith,
However great our zeal;
When others speak of life and death,
Let us not plunge a steel
Into the heart of one who talks
In terms we deem unorthodox.

Help us to send our thoughts through space,
Where worlds in trillions roll,
Each fashioned for its time and place,
Each portion of the whole;
Till our weak minds may feel a sense
Of Thy Supreme Omnipotence.

Let us not shame Thee with a creed
That builds a costly church,
But blinds us to a brother's need
Because he dares to search
For truth in his own soul and heart
And finds his church in home and mart.

Give us the faith that makes us kind,
Give us the open sight and mind
O God, the often mind
That lifts itself to meet the Ray
Of the New Dawning Day:
Lord, let us pray.

BE NOT DISMAYED
Be not dismayed, be not dismayed when death
Sets its white seal upon some worshipped face.
Poor human nature for a little space
Must suffer anguish, when that last drawn breath
Leaves such long silence; but let not thy faith
Fail for a moment in God's boundless grace.
But know, oh know, He has prepared a place
Fairer for our dear dead than worlds beneath,
Yet not beneath; for those entrancing spheres
Surround our earth as seas a barren isle.
Ours is the region of eternal fears;
Theirs is the region where God's radiant smile
Shines outward from the centre, and gives hope
Even to those who in the shadows grope.
They are not far from us. At first though long
And lone may seem the paths that intervene,
If ever on the staff of prayer we lean
The silence will grow eloquent with song
And our weak faith with certitude wax strong.
Intense, yet tranquil; fervent, yet serene,
He must be who would contact World Unseen
And comrade with their Amaranthine throng;
Not through the tossing waves of surging grief
Come spirit-ships to port. When storms subside,
Then with their precious cargoes of relief
Into the harbour of the heart they glide.
For him who will believe and trust and wait
Death's austere silence grows articulate.

ASCENSION
I have been down in the darkest water
Deep, deep down where no light could pierce;
Alone with the things that are bent on slaughter,
The mindless things that are cruel and fierce.
I have fought with fear in my wave-walled prison,
And begged for the beautiful boon of death;
But out of the billows my soul has risen

To glorify God with my latest breath.

There is no potion I have not tasted
Of all the bitters in life's large store;
And never a drop of the gall was wasted
That the lords of Karma saw fit to pour,
Though I cried as my Elder Brother before me,
'Father in heaven, let pass this cup!'
And the only response from the still skies o'er me
Was the brew held close for my lips to sup.

Yet I have grown strong on the gall Elysian,
And a courage has come that all things dares;
And I have been given an inner vision
Of the wonderful world where my dear one fares;
And I have had word from the great Hereafter
A marvellous message that throbs with truth,
And mournful weeping has changed to laughter,
And grief has changed into the joy of youth.

Oh! there was a time when I supped sweet potions,
And lightly uttered profound belief,
Before I went down in the swirling oceans
And fought with madness and doubt and grief.
Now I am climbing the Hills of Knowledge,
And I speak unfearing, and say 'I know,'
Though it be not to church, or to book, or college,
But to God Himself that my debt I owe.

For the ceaseless prayer of a soul is heeded,
When the prayer asks only for light and faith;
And the faith and the light and the knowledge needed
Shall gild with glory the path to death.
Oh! heart of the world by sorrow shaken,
Hear ye the message I have to give:
The seal from the lips of the dead is taken,
And they can say to you, 'Lo! we live.'

THE DEADLIEST SIN

There are not many sins when once we sift them.
In actions of evolving human souls
Striving to reach high goals
And falling backward into dust and mire,
Some element we find that seems to lift them
Above our condemnation, even higher
Into the realm of pity and compassion.

So beauteous a thing as love itself can fashion
A chain of sins; descending to desire,
It wanders into dangerous paths, and leads
To most unholy deeds,
And light-struck, walks in madness toward the night.

Wrong oft-times is an over-ripened right,
A rank weed grown from some neglected flower,
The lightning uncontrolled: flames meant for joy
And beauty, used to ravage and destroy.
For sins like these repentance can atone.
There is one sin alone
Which seems all unforgivable, because
It springs from no temptation and no need
And no desire, save to make sweet faith bleed,
And to defame God's laws.
Oh! viler than the murderer or the thief
Who slays the body and who robs the purse,
Is he who strives to kill the mind's belief
And rob it of its hope
Of life beyond this little pain-filled span.
God has no curse
Quite dark enough to punish such a man,
Who, seeing how souls grope
And suffer in this world of mighty losses,
And how hearts stagger on beneath life's crosses,
Yet strives to rob them of their staff of faith
And make them think dark death
Ends all existence; think the worshipped child
Cold in its mother's arms is but a clod
And has not gone to God;
That souls united by love undefiled
And holy can by death be torn asunder
To meet no more.
It must be true that under
This earth of ours there lies a Purgatory
For those who seek to rob grief of the glory
That shines through hope of life immortal. In
Sin's lexicon this is the vilest sin
Needless and cruel, ugly, gaunt and mean,
Without one poor excuse on which to lean,
A vandal sin, that with no hope of gain
Finds pleasure only in another's pain.

God! though all other sins on earth persist,
Strike dumb the blatant, loud-mouthed atheist.

THE RAINBOW OF PROMISE

In the face of the sun are great thunderbolts hurled,
And the storm-clouds have shut out its light;
But a Rainbow of Promise now shines on the world,
And the universe thrills at the sight.

'Tis the flag of our Union, the red, white, and blue,
Our Star-spangled Banner, our pride;
Fair symbol of all that is noble and true,
Flung out over continents wide.

Flung out in its glory o'er land and o'er sea,
With a message from God in each star;
And a glorious promise of peace yet to be
In the fluttering folds of each bar.

A Rainbow of Promise, bright emblem of hope,
Fair flag of each cause that is just;
No longer in doubt or in darkness we grope
In the Star-spangled Banner we trust.

THEY SHALL NOT WIN

Whatever the strength of our foes is now,
Whatever it may have been,
This is our slogan, and this our vow
They shall not win, they shall not win.

Though out of the darkness they call the aid
Of the evil forces of Sin,
We utter our slogan unafraid
They shall not win, they shall not win.

We know we are right, and know they are wrong,
So to God above and within
We make our vow and we sing our song
They shall not win, they shall not win.

It rises over the shriek of shell,
And over the cannons' din:
Our slogan shall scatter the hosts of Hell
They shall not win, they shall not win.

Ella Wheeler Wilcox – A Short Biography

Ella Wheeler was born on 5th November, 1850, on a farm in the village of Johnstown, Rock County, Wisconsin. Her parents, Marcus H. Wheeler and Sarah Pratt Wheeler, already had three children. A year earlier the family had moved from Vermont after Marcus's attempts at show business failed and becoming a farmer was his response. With Ella's birth they moved again. This time further north to Madison.

Ella was a gifted child, writing poetry and novels from an early age. The family was poor but her parents believed in education, and whilst little could be afforded they helped as best they could most usefully with grammar, spelling and vocabulary. Her initial education was at the local district school in the village of Windsor, now re-named in her honour as Ella Wheeler Wilcox School.

During her thirteenth year subscriptions the family had been receiving from the New York Mercury, a popular periodical, ceased. This greatly upset her. Life on the farm was lonely and the magazine had been a source of comfort and information about the big world beyond the farm. The family could not afford its own subscription so Ella had to make other plans.

Her writing ambitions were central to this. She wrote two essays but now had to obtain stamps so she could get her submissions in front of editors. She was corresponding with a young girl, Jean, who was in the freshman class at Madison University. Assuring her friend of future payment she enclosed the letter and essays for the New York Mercury.

By 1866, Jean, at Ella's behest, sent a list of all the monthlies and weeklies on the newsstands and Ella was hard at work saving pennies for postage as she began to mail them en masse with her works. Quickly her family lent their support to help out with her endeavours. Ella's mother especially had always thought her daughter would be the one to find the fame, travel and recognition that she had wanted herself and seeing the efforts Ella was putting in she was only to glad to help.

Soon the house the house was filled with ALL the periodicals. Editors would send magazines, books, pictures, bric-a-brac and tableware in response to Ella's requests and works. Being able to earn these items brought her great satisfaction and honed her skills.

She remembers the period in her autobiography:

"The very first verses I sent for publication were unmercifully "guyed" by my beloved "Mercury." The editor urged me to keep to prose and to avoid any further attempts at rhyme. He said that, while this criticism would wound me temporarily, it would eventually confer a favour on me and the world at large.

"My first check came from Frank Leslie's publishing house. I wrote asking for one of his periodicals to be sent to me in return for three little poems I had composed in one day. In reply came a check for ten dollars, saying I must select which one of some thirteen publications they issued at that time.

This bit of crisp paper opened a perfect floodgate of aspiration, inspiration and ambition for me. I had not thought of earning money so soon. I had expected to obtain only books, magazines and articles of use and beauty from the editor's prize-lists; and I had not supposed verses to be saleable. I wrote them because they came to me, but I expected to be a novelist like Mrs. Southworth and May Agens Fleming in time - that was the goal of my dreams. The check from Leslie was a revelation. I walked, talked, thought and dreamed in verse after that. A day which passed without a poem from my pen I considered lost and misused. Two each day was my idea of industry, and I once achieved eight. They sold, the majority, for three dollars or five dollars each. Sometimes I got ten dollars for a poem, that was always an event. Short love-stories, over which I laboured painfully, as story writing was an acquired habit, also added to my income, bringing me ten or fifteen dollars, and once in a while larger sums, from "Peterson's," "Demorest's," "Harper's Bazaar" and the "Chimney Corner."

Ella was beginning to understand the route to success and had the work ethic and creativity to turn it to her advantage. Ella would write her daily quota of poems and other works and then send them out to editors in the hope of getting them published.

It was also about this time that she also left the Country school. Her record in grammar, spelling, reading had of course been excellent but she had a horror of mathematics preferring to spend as much time as possible in the world of her imagination. Ella's talent and determination was such that by now, after she graduated from High School she was already well known in her state as a young writer.

In this she was encouraged by her mother, who despised her own life and felt herself and her family superior to all her neighbours and was forever impressing on the young teenager that her life would blossom and she would achieve success as a writer.

In 1867 her parents sent her to Madison where she was a junior in the Female College, a part of the University of Wisconsin. Ella wanted to spend all of her time writing and begged to come home. She didn't feel the need for further education and was painfully aware of the difference between her homemade clothes and the dresses of city girl. These and other differences caused her to feel left out and not part of the group. After many requests her parents relented and she was allowed home to continue her writing.

In 1870 she was offered employment at $45 a month to edit the literary department of a publication by the magazine's Milwaukee Editor. She accepted, but the hours and work were not to her liking and after three months the magazine folded and her single experience of working in an office was over. Now she was to be a full time author.

In 1872 she published her first book. It was an unusual step as it was a book of poems entitled 'Drops Of Water: Poems' that were solely about abstinence. Published by the National Temperance society it reflected her views on the evils of alcohol and earned her a $50 fee.

She published further books over the next decade but it wasn't until 1883 and the rather racy, for those times, publication of Poems of Passion that her success moved suddenly forward. It was an immediate and large scale success selling over 60,000 in two years.

That same year was also noteworthy for she was engaged to be married. Robert Wilcox was one of many suitors to the young Ella. He was a silver salesman from Meriden, Connecticut. Although they only met three times before the wedding it was to be the relationship that defined her life and much of her work. They married the following year in 1884.

Her most famous poem, "Solitude", was first published on 25th February, 1883 in an issue of The New York Sun. The inspiration for the poem came as she was travelling to attend the State Governor's inaugural ball in Madison, Wisconsin. Whilst travelling to the celebration she was sitting next to a young woman, dressed in black, who was in obvious distress. Ella comforted her for the whole journey. Recalling the widow's emotional state Ella wrote:

Laugh, and the world laughs with you;
Weep, and you weep alone.
For the sad old earth must borrow its mirth
But has trouble enough of its own

She sent the poem to the Sun and received $5 for her effort. It was collected in the book Poems of Passion shortly after in May 1883.

The newlyweds lived for a short time in Robert's home town of Meriden, Connecticut, before moving to New York City and then to Granite Bay in the Short Beach area of Branford, Connecticut. They built two homes and several cottages on Long Island Sound where they would hold gatherings of their literary and artistic friends.

On May 27, 1887, Ella gave birth to a son. Tragically he was only to survive for a few short hours.

In the early years of their marriage, they both developed an interest in theosophy, New Thought, and spiritualism. As this developed Robert and Ella Wheeler Wilcox promised each other that whoever died first would return and attempt to communicate with the other.

Ella had by now published many books of poetry as well as novels and other writings. Her writing life was filled with success on a national scale. Some volumes were collections based on a theme others on a particular time. Some of her war poetry that centred on the Great War in Europe is quite compelling. As she was never considered literary but rather mass market a lot of her work has not received the recognition that other lesser writers have obtained.

In 1916 after thirty years of marriage Robert Wilcox died. Ella was naturally devastated and desperate. Rather than dissipate her grief seemed to grow ever more intense as the days and weeks went by with no message from him. She journeyed to California to see the Rosicrucian astrologer, Max Heindel, seeking help in her sorrow as to why she had no word from Robert. She writes:

"In talking with Max Heindel, the leader of the Rosicrucian Philosophy in California, he made very clear to me the effect of intense grief. Mr. Heindel assured me that I would come in touch with the spirit of my husband when I learned to control my sorrow. I replied that it seemed strange to me that an omnipotent God could not send a flash of his light into a suffering soul to bring its conviction when most needed. Did you ever stand beside a clear pool of water, asked Mr. Heindel, and see the trees and skies repeated therein? And did you ever cast a stone into that pool and see it clouded and turmoiled, so it gave no reflection? Yet the skies and trees were waiting above to be reflected when the waters grew calm. So God and your husband's spirit wait to show themselves to you when the turbulence of sorrow is quieted".

It seemed good advice. She wrote herself a short affirmative prayer to help calm her inner turmoil and would repeat it to herself over and over:

"I am the living witness: The dead live: And they speak through us and to us: And I am the voice that gives this glorious truth to the suffering world: I am ready, God: I am ready, Christ: I am ready, Robert."

She had already written in 1915 a booklet 'What I Know About New Thought which had sold over 50,000 copies. These and other books on New Thought, together with her expanding efforts to educate a wider audience to the powers of positive thinking, were a great comfort to her.

Ella expresses this unique blend of New Thought, Spiritualism and Reincarnation with these powerful words:

"As we think, act, and live here today, we built the structures of our homes in spirit realms after we leave earth, and we build karma for future lives, thousands of years to come, on this earth or other planets. Life will assume new dignity, and labour new interest for us, when we come to the knowledge that death is but a continuation of life and labour, in higher planes".

Ella fell ill in France in early 1919. It was breast cancer. She was taken initially to England and then back to her home. She died of the cancer on October 31, 1919.

Her final words in her autobiography 'The Worlds and I' were:

"From this mighty storehouse (of God, and the hierarchies of Spiritual Beings) we may gather wisdom and knowledge, and receive light and power, as we pass through this preparatory room of earth, which is only one of the innumerable mansions in our Father's house. Think on these things".

A Concise Bibliography
1872   Drops of water, poems.
1873   Shells.
1876   Maurine.
1883   Poems of Passion.
1886   Mal Moule'e, a novel.
1886   Perdita, and other stories.
1888   The Adventures of Miss Volney.
1888   Poems of Pleasure.
1891   A Double Life.
1891   How Salvator Won, and other recitations.
1892   Was it Suicide?
1892   The Beautiful Land of Nod.
1892   An Erring Woman's Love.
1892   Sweet Danger.
1893   The Song of the Sandwich.
1893   Men, Women and Emotions.
1896   An Ambitious Man.
1896   Custer, and other poems.

1897	Three Women.
1897	Roger Merritt's Crime.
1901	Every-day Thoughts in Prose and Verse.
1901	Poems of Power.
1902	The Heart of the New Thought.
1902	Kingdom of Love and How Salvator Won.
1902	The Other Woman's Husband.
1902	Poems of Life.
1904	Around the Year with Ella Wheeler Wilcox.
1904	A Woman of the World.
1905	Mizpah; or, the story of Esther, poetical drama in four acts.
1905	Poems of Love.
1905	Poems of Reflection.
1905	The Story of a literary career.
1906	Poems of Sentiment.
1906	New Thought pastels.
1906	Poems of Peace.
1907	The Kingdom of love, and other poems.
1907	The Love Sonnets of Abelard and Heloise.
1908	New Thought - common sense and what life means to me.
1908	Poems of Cheer.
1908	Selected Poems.
1909	Poems of Progress and New Thought Pastels.
1909	Sailing Sunny Seas.
1910	Diary of a Faithless Husband.
1910	The New Hawaiian Girl; a play.
1910	Poems of Experience.
1910	Yesterdays.
1911	Are you Alive?
1912	Picked Poems.
1912	Gems from Ella Wheeler Wilcox.
1912	The Englishman and other Poems.
1914	Poems of Problems.
1914	The art of Being Alive.
1914	Cameos.
1914	Lest we Forget.
1914	Poems of Ella Wheeler Wilcox.
1915	Poems of Optimism.
1916	World Voices.
1916	More Poems.
1916	Poems of Purpose.
1917	Poetical Works of Ella Wheeler Wilcox.
1918	Sonnets of Sorrow and Triumph.
1918	The Worlds and I.
1919	Poems.
1919	Cinema Poems and others.
1919	Hello Boys!

Published Posthumously
1920   Poems of Affection.
1920   Great Thoughts For Each Day's Life.
1924   Collected Poems of Ella Wheeler Wilcox.
1927   Gems from E.W.Wilcox

www.ingramcontent.com/pod-product-compliance
Lightning Source LLC
Chambersburg PA
CBHW061259040426

42444CB00010B/2428